# Dalek

# Christianity

# Dalek

# Christianity

## Empathy and Understanding the Bible

**Tom Schwarz**

Published by The Invisible Imprint in the United Kingdom in 2023

ISBN: 978-1-83919-523-5

I would like to thank Marcus and Wendy Pawsey, leaders of my church gathering in Princes Risborough for encouraging me to write and providing opportunities to improve my public speaking, and actually believe I have something to contribute. I would like to thank Craig Sumption, who let me loose on his group in Johannesburg to road test some of the material. Thanks to Ian and Jenny Gray for encouragement and being willing to be interviewed. Thanks to my wife for her piercing insights.

# Contents

# Purpose of the book

Why should a Christian book be called *Dalek Christianity*? Is there anything Christian about the Daleks? They had a particular aspect of their evil which was intolerant of anything not exactly the same as them. Anything remotely different was to be exterminated. It is very easy to look at these aliens and condemn them out of hand. But do they ask us a question? Is there something of the Dalek in all of us? If you still have no idea what I'm on about, another way of looking at it – actually, this could have been an alternative title – is applying the statement 'I'm a heretic and so are you!'.

Perhaps the word 'heretic' is a bit strong. Here is a definition: 'heretic noun [C]: someone who has an opinion that is opposite to or against the official or popular opinion' (https://dictionary.cambridge.org/dictionary/english/heretic).

Within Christianity there have been a number of official or popular opinions about heresy that have varied over the centuries. To give an example, Pentecostal Christianity was officially seen as a heresy and took a long time to be accepted as a valid expression of the faith by the church at large. Most people

1

agree it started at the Azusa Street Revival in 1906, but Pentecostals were not accepted as members of the American Association of Evangelicals until 1943. So what was once supposed heresy does not always have to remain so.

The thing about church history that makes me sad, is that when someone discovers a new or slightly different perspective on the faith it often takes a long time for that point of view to be appreciated.

These days the church seems to be fragmented as never before, even though there are more opportunities to be together than ever before, thanks to international travel and the Internet. We could spend ages analysing why this is so, but this book is more about finding some practical ways to help.

Think about the statement: 'We are all heretics.' I don't know what thoughts went through your head. Maybe some of the following:

'Well, I know some heretics but not me.'

'Time to stop reading this book.'

'I'm not a heretic. I follow the official teaching on everything.'

'So, are you going to show me how not to be a heretic? 'Cos I don't want to be!'

'But aren't heretics all bad people who don't believe the truth and have broken away from the church?'

Chances are one or more of the above thoughts came into your mind. That's OK. Let me now suggest a perspective that will help you to decide if you want to come on this journey with me. If you are still uncomfortable with the term 'heretic', please feel free to leave it behind. Seeing faith from multiple perspectives is what I am actually trying to say (but that's quite a long phrase).

The scripture says, 'We have the mind of Christ' (1 Corinthians 2:16, *NIV*). This, at least, means that believers as a community (*we* not *I*) are able to understand something about Christ and what His intentions are for humanity. However, does it mean that all believers at all times in history must think and act in exactly the same way? I think not.

I think you will agree that the mind of God is unlimited, but that our minds are limited. Yet, by the gift of God, we are given the ability of awareness of the divine. This awareness varies from person to person, depending on so many factors. Some of these factors are cultural, some are intellectual, some are linked to personality preferences, and some are a result of the period of history we find ourselves in. I remember someone came up to me once, after a church meeting, and said, 'When you play, I can feel the presence of angels.' That was a very nice thing to say, but I had been playing a Roland keyboard with some nice celestial keypad sounds. If I'd had a honky-tonk piano instead what would she have felt? Something to do with the hokey-cokey, maybe?

We are limited in our perspectives. So are other people, but their limitations may be different from ours. Shall we start a journey to look at other perspectives and celebrate differences? Are we all heretics to some extent? Let's make our lives richer as we explore together.

You can read this book from beginning to end if you want (I can't stop you!). However, I have put a few questions to consider at the end of each chapter. You can read these on your own or with any kind of group. If you are leading a group, I have made it easy by providing some suggested answers to the questions if no one can think of anything to say. Often hearing a similar story will enable people to dig out something from the recesses of their minds. At the end of the book each chapter has a notes section to provide some guidance.

# Your struggles are different from other people's

There's an old song by Randy Stonehill that I used to listen to a lot (in 1979!). It had a line that implied we were all the same, and that that was the basis of how we were to live. I used to think that everyone was like me and believed we all needed life to have significance and meaning. For me, that was why Jesus came and died. Anything else was irrelevant: healing (nope, I'm well, thanks), provision (no, I'm OK, got a student grant – oh yes, back in the day), forgiveness of sins (well, I have a few, I suppose), life eternal (thanks, but that's a way off, isn't it?). Of course, what was happening there was that Jesus was meeting me at my point of need, as He always does. Other people have different needs, and Jesus meets them at those points.

Our points of need are different. So when we are talking about how Jesus meets our needs, they will be different needs. I know this is blindingly obvious, but I want to unpack the idea and then work out what is a good way to share our faith and our testimony with people who have a different life story to ours. I have often heard people say you can't argue with a testimony, as it is real, whereas you can argue with arguments. There is some truth in that, but ultimately a testimony is personal and may strike a chord with one person but not necessarily with another. That is not to deny the reality of your testimony, but it may have more relevance to certain types of people who can relate to it.

Let me give an example. I recently found out that most people do *not* have a constant stream of junk – random and sometimes plain stupid or evil thoughts – assailing their brains every waking hour (and don't mention weird dreams). Although this might be an aspect of ADHD, which I possibly have, it is a point of need for me. There are several aspects of biblical teaching and spiritual concepts that I find extremely helpful and relevant as a result. In his second letter to the Corinthians, Paul asks us to take every thought captive and make it obedient to Christ:

> We demolish arguments and every pretension that
> sets itself up against the knowledge of God, and we
> take captive every thought to make it obedient to
> Christ.

> (2 Corinthians 10:5, *NIV*)

This I have to do as a discipline pretty much all the time. I have learned not to consider these thoughts my own but to consider them an aspect of mental activity that I have to learn to control, through the power of the Holy Spirit and knowledge of the Bible.

Here are a few examples from my racing brain: while driving along, I get the thought, 'Why not drive straight into the car opposite?' Or I imagine a scenario where someone is making fun of me and when I overreact to this the scene develops into a violent horror movie (if I let it). I see a juxtaposition between two words and immediately want to make a very inappropriate pun. (I often don't win the battle on this one.) I have, in the past, mentioned this tendency to others. Some have looked at me like I'm weird. They don't have this struggle. Taking every thought captive is not an issue for them.

Now let's look at an opposite example. Jesus tells us not to worry in his sermon on the mount, and He gives good reasons:

Therefore I tell you, do not worry about your life,
what you will eat or drink; or about your body, what
you will wear. Is not life more than food, and the
body more than clothes? 26 Look at the birds of the
air; they do not sow or reap or store away in barns,
and yet your heavenly Father feeds them. Are you not
much more valuable than they? 27 Can any one of you
by worrying add a single hour to your life?

(Matthew 6:25–27, *NIV*)

Now I have never been one to worry. Even when I was an unbeliever I never really got scared of anything. The only time I was a bit concerned was when I got left in the middle of the main road from Bury to Manchester on a dark evening with solid lines of traffic coming both ways. My friends had run between two cars leaving me stuck. I had a very worrying thirty seconds before I found a gap in the traffic and was able to run to safety. At the age of thirteen I flew from San Francisco to Manchester as an unaccompanied minor without even thinking about what might happen. (There was a two-hour layover at JFK Airport where I hung out in the business lounge and chatted to a couple of British businessmen. They asked me which part of the States I was from.) However, many of us live with worry and it is an almost all-consuming emotion. Matthew 6 provides reassurance and gives a worried person something to meditate on.

So what should we make of this? Certainly, we should be ready to share our testimony of what God has done for us, and it will often strike a chord. But we need to be aware that if our testimony is not having an impact, this is not because it is invalid or that we have failed in any way. It could be that it is just not scratching where the other person is itching.

## Questions for discussion

1. What was one main issue that brought you to faith?
2. What sort of issues would bring others to faith?

## Hints for leaders

If people are quiet, give some examples in addition to reading the chapter. You could:

### 1. Ask how many people

- are afraid of death.
- have questions about the meaning of life.
- are in financial, health or relationship difficulties.
- are in need of guidance.
- feel unvalued.
- feel lost.

- need a purpose.

## 2. Tell this story as an example

The people of Santrokofi in south-eastern Ghana would often get themselves into debt putting on huge funerals for their dear departed. This was mainly because they believed the dead would go to the ancestors. The first question the ancestors would ask of the dead was, 'Did you get a good send-off?' If the answer was no, then they believed the ancestors would call the funeral organiser and talk to him. The funeral organiser would then have to go and meet with the ancestors, which of course meant he would have to die. The truth that the ancestors cannot have this kind of hold over anyone will speak powerfully to someone who used to be in fear of their ancestors but is no longer because of the liberating power of the gospel. Different people have different needs. If you have a testimony of financial provision it might be interpreted differently by someone with this background. Their debt issues may well be linked to what they believe about their ancestors.

# The Bible is one book for all people in all ages

Some of the Bible may not say much to you now, but it may have meant a lot to another culture in another time. First, take a moment to reflect how much we would know about God without the Bible. I know that historically people with no previous knowledge of Jesus have had very vivid dreams and visions of him, and I am not doubting for a minute that these experiences were real.

However, I think it is clear that without some knowledge of the Bible any beliefs we have about how the world began, what it will develop into, how we can live eternally or who we are as human beings will be extremely vague.

At the other extreme, if we were to take everything in the Bible literally, we would not be wearing cotton and polyester shirts, as this would go against Levitical law. Just hold the but, but, buts for a moment …

Consider this: John 1 says, 'The Word became flesh and lived among us.' Jesus the eternal Son of God became human and entered this world at a specific point in history. (Thankfully the Bible tells us it was 'just at the right time' (Romans 5:6, NIV).) Inevitably, there will be differences of opinion among us as to how much of the culture of that time we should follow to be good disciples of Jesus. There will also be different parts of scripture that resonate with people dependent on the age or culture in which they find themselves.

Here are a couple of examples. The first example is from my time in Ghana, where my family and I lived with the Mamprusi people. The Mamprusis love their kingly line, and their paramount chief is only eligible for the position if he can trace his ancestry back fourteen generations. In the genealogy of Jesus, He traces his ancestry back three times fourteen generations. How relevant is this to someone in an individualistic Western culture? Not much. But it is relevant to someone for whom kingship is important, and it shows that Jesus is King of Kings in a relatable way.

My second example is that many people react with disgust to the story where Jesus healed a blind man by spitting on the ground and rubbing the mud into his eyes. It just doesn't sit well with a society that values cleanliness. But there are certain groups in South America whose healers use this technique, and who are even referred to as 'spitters'. So Jesus is communicated to them as the 'chief spitter'.

So how does this affect our Bible reading? It is always good to know as much Bible background as possible. This can help us unlock meanings and find out exactly why early Christians were asked to do things in a certain way. This may have made sense for them then, but does it now? We need to recognise that today we may come to different conclusions.

One key passage to look at is Acts 15. At that time the church was growing and large numbers of non-Jews were joining. The crucial issue was whether these new believers should follow Jewish law or not. A council was convened, and they came up with three rules for these new believers to follow: (1) don't eat food sacrificed to idols; (2) don't eat blood; (3) don't sleep around. These were widely accepted, although the Apostle Paul had to continue to encourage believers not to go back to full observance of the Jewish law as a way to walk with God.

A few years ago, I did a social media post and explained about these three rules for new believers back in the day. I asked what three rules people would suggest now. Of course the answers given were varied and different. One person even suggested no rules at all.

The point is that over time there will be different emphases on what rules are important to follow. This should come as no surprise, as the story of the Bible is an unfolding one: it began in a garden but ends in a city. Our pilgrimage is not back to the garden but onward to the city.

Through the ages the church has lived alongside different prevailing philosophies and political climates. No one can deny that we are affected by the times in which we live. I live in a modern Western society. I expect healthcare and education for my children. I expect to operate in a society which takes taxes and distributes benefits. I expect God to work in this situation. Recently, a family member was granted financial support for their disability, and this was seen as an answer to prayer. Where I lived in Ghana these support systems did not exist.

We will constantly be wrestling with a timeless and eternal God who, through the ongoing presence of the Holy Spirit, lives among us and can relate to whatever society we are in.

## Questions for discussion

1. What verses or passages do you remember that don't really resonate with you?

2. How could these passages be applied somewhere else? Perhaps convert them into a form that you can relate to. For example, take a parable that is about farming (e.g. the sower) and make it more technological.

# Hints for leaders

Here is the parable of the sower converted to an online advertising context. Use this if no one can think of their own examples.

A solar panel manufacturer wanted to sell as many panels as possible. He paid for world-wide online advertising. Some of the advertising was targeted at an area that didn't even have the Internet, so it was completely wasted. Some of the advertising reached an organisation that bought hundreds of panels but couldn't find anyone to install them, so the panels were unused. Some of the advertising reached people who bought panels and installed them, but their area was so cloudy they hardly got any power at all. But some advertising reached people who installed their panels in the sunshine and even had enough electricity to share with their neighbours.

# Chart your belief: how our perspectives vary

All of us in our idle moments have done one of those social media quizzes that asks a few questions and then tells you what brand of Christian you are (oh, only me, oh well). These narrow things down to a few categories by taking the largest number of answers you selected that fit a particular denominational viewpoint and ignoring the rest. This is a bit of fun and, of course, a gross oversimplification.

Have you ever wondered, within the spectrum of Christian belief, how many differing points of view there are? Have you ever thought that you have to get it right somehow, in order to qualify for blessings from God or approval from your denomination or tribe or whatever?

In John 17, Jesus talks to His disciples in the Upper Room prior to his death and resurrection. He says a prayer for those in the future:

My prayer is not for them [the twelve disciples] alone.

I pray also for those who will believe in me through

their message, 21 that all of them may be one, Father,

just as you are in me and I am in you. May they also

be in us so that the world may believe that you have

sent me. 22 I have given them the glory that you gave

me, that they may be one as we are one – 23 I in them

and you in me – so that they may be brought to

complete unity. Then the world will know that you

sent me and have loved them even as you have loved

me.

(John 17:20–23, *NIV*)

Jesus is praying for you and me right now in the twenty-first century. We are not doing very well at answering His prayer. In this section, I want to explore why this may be and (spoiler alert) suggest that everyone believing the same thing is not the answer to his prayer. In most cases, the Bible gives us examples of people praying *to* God, and we can learn how to pray by following those examples. Here Jesus is praying *for* us. If we pray to God we expect Him to answer. In this case we are the answer to Jesus's prayer. I find this quite amazing.

I am going to list a wide selection of issues on which Christians differ. These have changed over the centuries. Many of these questions do not have one definite answer because there is a spectrum of belief. Some of these issues are paradoxical, i.e. both are true even though one seems to go against the other. It is not my purpose to provide answers for this – many others have done that better than I ever could.

Now, it may be that you have not spent any significant amount of time pondering a particular issue but, by aligning yourself with a specific group, you have assented to accept a load of principles as a block. When I first became a believer after a period of existential agnosticism a friend who was of a more traditional denomination asked if I now believed in a literal Adam and Eve. 'I haven't really thought about it but I suppose so,' I answered. Over time I have thought about this and have concluded that my friend's assumption was that *all* Bible-believing Christians interpreted Genesis literally.

I am not going to comment in detail on the compatibility of a whole block of beliefs lumped into one but here are some thoughts. These beliefs could be influenced by your denomination, your culture, your political affiliation, or the nation you live in. Do you want an example? OK, you've twisted my arm. In the UK, the vast majority of believers don't hold an opinion on exactly how Christ will return, although they believe He will. In the USA, there are churches that insist on members having a particular belief about this as a prerequisite of membership. So there is a national difference. It would be interesting to delve into the history of this, but because I know little about it I've kept my example deliberately vague just to give you an idea of what I'm talking about.

Listed below are some beliefs that we Christians disagree on, sometimes very mildly, sometimes quite violently. At various points in history, groups have decided to condemn one another as heretical, and the same happens today. (Just to state my basic point of view, I believe that the Bible is true and that the creeds of the church through the ages are also true, though there is so much more to be discovered.)

### Theological beliefs

- What is the problem of evil? This is the one we are often quizzed about. Are our answers to this question rather glib? Is our viewpoint more Augustinian or dualistic?
- Are spiritual gifts for today? Or did they cease with the apostles?
- What is the end condition of unbelievers?
- Are we spirit, soul and body, or just soul and body?
- Do we like Hebrew-type thinking or Greek-type thinking?
- Does God hate us? How much?
- Who is saved?

### Appropriate practices for Christians

- Divorce

- LGBTQ questions
- Role of women
- Environmentalism (i.e. should we be environmentalists or just wait for God to save us once this old planet wears out?)

## How Christians relate to the world

- Creation in six days with a young Earth, or God using evolution and the world being billions of years old?
- Baptism of children or only of believers?
- Eucharist – open or closed? Do unbelievers benefit in any way?
- Eucharist – memorial, real or transubstantiated?
- To what extent should we apply Christian morality to society?
- Spectrums of belief.
- Cultural ranking of acceptable and unacceptable sins.
- The order of believing, behaving and belonging with reference to the church.
- The extent to which different sections of the Bible are:
  - narrative.
  - a principle to be interpreted for the times in which it was given.
  - something even more relevant now than it was at the time of writing.

o   guidelines to be followed for all time.

I have listed twenty-four areas where Christians differ. These will vary at different points in history. Now imagine you are free to have your opinion on all twenty-four of these areas. Most likely you will find yourself somewhere along the spectrum of belief rather than at one extreme or the other. Despite this, the number of people you would have to meet before you found someone who shared exactly the same opinion as you could be two to the power of twenty-four (16,777,216). There are about 40,000 denominations worldwide, by the way. At least there aren't 16 million!

So when Jesus prayed for unity was this an impossible prayer? I don't think so. Jesus also said, 'You will know the truth and the truth will set you free' (John 8.32, *NIV*). I think, being part of Jesus's community is more organic, and that this will look different for you than it does for someone else. Your Jesus-focused community might look like something that focuses on a church building or it may look more like a network of relationships. Traditional creeds talk about 'the communion of the saints', but wisely they do not specify what that communion looks like.

Over the years, I have experienced different denominations, ways of worshipping and ways of relating to God. One of my formative experiences was at a church where I was part of a team who encouraged others to experience God more deeply.

This was back in the previous millennium. (You would love to know which church and who led the group and what their angle on various issues was, wouldn't you?) Anyway, we led the meetings on Saturday and also on Sunday morning and had an amazing time. We had never seen people more hungry for the presence of God. On Sunday evening, apart from delivering the message, the service was scheduled to be led by the local church, not by us. The format was extremely high church and traditional, which we were not expecting at all. This uplifting experience has stayed with me and taught me never to judge a book by its cover. I personally don't go for traditional services and prefer modern, but I always need to remind myself that this is a preference.

I must confess I have never spent an extended amount of time worshipping at a church that was not my preferred one. In the questions below, I suggest different ways to do this.

To examine this idea further, here is a real-life example, taken from an interview with Jenny Gray, a Christian from a charismatic Pentecostal background. When Jenny was at university, she attended worship at an Anglican church.

### What were your expectations?
I guess I was expecting a lot more hymns. It was a big city church linked with Holy Trinity Brompton, and I'd been to High Anglican services as a child here and there. This was a

spirit-filled church, but although there was order, there was space for the Holy Spirit as well. I'd expected it to be more regimented. We had a lot of stand up and sit down – we would stand for about three songs and then sit down and say some lovely words – but it was not as much as I was expecting.

### What didn't you understand? Did you need explanation?

I wasn't familiar with some of the liturgy. But it wasn't like an Anglican church I went to in Swindon that had its own tunes for some of the service words, which I found very disconcerting. The church leaders were quite good at explaining who was going to say what, i.e. which words on the screen displaying the liturgy.

### Anything you did not like?

I didn't like real wine with communion as opposed to a tray with teeny tiny cups. We came to the front and we knelt at the 'bar'. We had the wine in a proper chalice like we were suppliants. [At this point Jenny had to be told the bar was called a chancel as she didn't know that was its name.] I didn't dislike that it was quite a physical act – it can feel a bit throwaway at a Pentecostal church – but it took forever with a church of two hundred people, and we all had to go up in turn.

### Anything very different that you preferred?

I used to find Anglican prayers a bit formulaic, but then I had a slot doing the prayers at this church, which were quite personal. People would spend time looking at the songs being picked, the time of year, the things going on in the news and the scriptures. Actually, there was a lot going into those prayer slots. People listened to the Holy Spirit as they prepared. It was more personal than I realised.

There is a wealth of Bible truth in the liturgical words that when spoken with truth are hugely impactful. As a result I value order more than I used to. The Holy Spirit can work through order. If you prepare three weeks in advance, the Holy Spirit still guides and leads you; you can still listen on the day and change your mind. But there were so many services where the worship leader, preacher and prayer slot person didn't know what content the others were bringing. However all the team's contributions came together on the morning, even though they had prepared different amounts of time beforehand.

## Questions for discussion

1. What are you doing to answer Jesus's prayer for unity?
2. Have you ever experienced a different denomination? If not, how can you make that happen?

- Could you take a short sabbatical from your own church and go somewhere different for a few months (not secretly of course)?
- Is there another church that has services that don't clash with yours?
- Church is not just about services. Could you volunteer your 'services' with another church? Maybe you have a gift that could actually be used elsewhere (do talk about this with your church leader before they think you're leaving for good!)
- Could you get involved in something inter-church like Churches Together or whatever there is in your area?

## Hints for leaders

I would not be surprised if most people had never seriously considered these questions. If so, you might want to explore whether people feel that their lives should consist, to some extent, of an answer to Jesus's prayer. Question two provides some possible options. You might need to think how these would work in your cultural situation.

Discuss different ways people celebrate their faith. Some people are blessed by visiting ancient churches. Others would want to be 'slain in the Spirit'. I personally prefer a good set of worship songs, preferably rock.

To explore this further maybe have a look at *Sacred Pathways* by Gary Thomas, which focuses on nine different types of spirituality. I don't think you need to read the whole book to get the idea.

If you don't get answers from your group, try suggesting the following as a way of talking to believers who follow a different tradition or way of faith: make sure you spend at least as much time listening to them about their experience as you do about your own. If the conversation gets stuck, ask them questions like: What do you appreciate about this? Am I missing out on anything?

# Are you monocultural or intercultural and why does it matter?

In Genesis 50 Joseph's father Jacob dies in Egypt, but to fulfil a sworn promise he is taken back to Israel to be buried in his tomb in Canaan. What I find interesting here is that he is given all the Egyptian embalming procedures, to such an extent that when the Canaanites see the funeral they comment, 'The Egyptians are holding a solemn ceremony of mourning' (Genesis 50:11, *NIV*). Joseph has been greatly used by God in Egypt and is sure of his identity as an Israelite. However, that doesn't stop him from taking on Egyptian customs that make the Canaanites mistake him for an Egyptian. The above quote seems to be a throwaway comment and I wonder why it is even mentioned as it doesn't seem to be essential to the story. But it gives us what I feel is a refreshing perspective on identity. Just because you have a particular core identity doesn't mean you can't be, or appreciate, something else in addition.

In 2 Chronicles 2:11–14, Hiram of Tyre sends along Hu-ram-abi to work on a temple. Huram-abi's mother is from Dan (a tribe of Israel) and his father is from Tyre. Nothing negative is said about his bicultural upbringing, just the fact that he is hugely talented in metalwork. Nothing negative is said about Hiram either, who recognises the goodness of God to Israel.

I wonder how many of us are basically monocultural and how many of us have two or more cultural heritages that form part of our identity. Often these identities can be hidden until you tease them out. I am part of a global worship band that plays God-focused songs in as many different styles and lan-guages as our audiences will put up with. We are normally in-vited to play in obviously multicultural settings. However, re-cently we were playing at a Baptist church in a small town in Bedfordshire. Some of the congregation were under the im-pression that everyone attending was basically English. As the service got under way we asked those present to shout out if they had any non-British heritage. There was a Korean lady, and there was a British-born guy with Jamaican parents who very much felt that his Jamaican heritage was part of who he was. We actually found out that about ten per cent of those attending were intercultural in some way.

We all know that our cultural heritage colours our lives and influences what we consider important, what we consider proper and what we consider good taste. (Well if you didn't know, now you do!) Of course it also affects how we interpret the scriptures. If we have only one culture in our lives we can identify it and fairly easily work out how it affects our interpretations. As an English person, for example, I struggle when people show up unannounced. However, hospitality in many cultures is straightforward and people expect to be able to pop in to others' houses any time. But someone who is monoculturally English might find the scriptural encouragement to show hospitality quite challenging. If you are monocultural, it could be quite difficult to adapt your habits. More to the point, it may be harder to see why people are behaving as they do or why they find different things important.

If you have more than one strong cultural influence or identity in your life, I think adapting to differences is easier. But for many of us, this is not the case. Either we do not come from an intercultural background, or we have not spent a significant amount of time living inside another culture.

So what happens when we see or hear another believer behaving in a way that we wouldn't? We could ask ourselves if there is a cultural element involved. Let me ground this in a scriptural example from a passage that people disagree about a lot: 1 Corinthians 11, which talks about the need for women to cover their heads in church. There has been every response imaginable to this passage, from ignoring the whole idea as completely culturally irrelevant to church today, to some places of worship where all the women wear headscarves. But then, I wonder to myself if they wear headscarves anyway rather than it being because of 1 Corinthians 11. (If you would like to explore this issue more deeply, there is a very interesting article on the significance of hairstyles in the Roman world – see resources section for details.)

Anyway, as you can tell by now, the aim of this book is not for me to express my opinion about a particular issue, but rather to ask how we can get along better when we all see things a little bit differently.

## Questions for discussion

1. Do you have an intercultural identity that you'd like to explore? If you don't know where to start:
   - Look at any family traditions or habits that are different from other people's. Where did they come from?
   - Look at your ancestors and see where they came from and any influences they might have had. How will you appreciate and celebrate any differences you come across?
2. What cultures do you have? Maybe try expressing them as a percentage. For example, I have always said I am a quarter German because of my grandfather, but then I

spent many years in Ghana, and that influences me as much as my Germanness, so maybe I would say I am seventy per cent English, ten per cent German, twenty per cent Ghanaian. Numbers don't matter much; this is just a way to explore.

3. How much of your biblical understanding is influenced by your own cultures? This is not a question you can answer straight away. Maybe it is one to take away and ponder as you study passages of scripture.

## Hints for leaders

If people in the group feel they all are the same culture, you could start to explore regional differences. Perhaps ask which football team they support. I once revealed I had a preference for a certain team and a fellow Christian started being very tribal and pretended to vomit. It was a joke but it revealed divisions, nonetheless.

It is quite possible that people will talk about church cultures. Encourage participants to say positive things about church cultures that they are not a part of. Go back to the interview with Jenny Gray in the previous chapter.

You could also talk about this in terms of places where people have lived for extended periods of time. Tell this example story: in most European countries, marriage ceremonies take place in a registry office. Christians then celebrate the wedding additionally in a church setting. In the UK most Christian weddings take place in church and the minister is also a registrar. The European model often comes as a shock to British Christians. But the fact remains that if you have just a church wedding in Germany you are seen as unmarried in the eyes of the state.

# The limitations of language

The prophet Ezekiel was privileged to see some amazing visions of supernatural beings. He recorded his impressions for us in chapter one. It is an amazing vision of heaven and of the glory of God, very similar to that experienced by John in Revelation 1. What they both saw was real and is a foretaste of the immense glory that is to come, prepared for us by God our Father.

Ezekiel's vision is communicated to us through written language, not audio or video. If you speak ancient Hebrew you can read the actual words. Most of us have to rely on a translation. I'm going to use the *ESV* (*English Standard Version*) because the translation is quite literal but uses modern English. This is because I would like us to think about the actual vocabulary that Ezekiel had at his disposal to describe something that was out of this world:

> As I looked, behold, a stormy wind came out of the
> north, and a great cloud, with brightness around it,
> and fire flashing forth continually, and in the midst of
> the fire, as it were gleaming metal.

(Ezekiel 1:4, *ESV*)

Ezekiel would have been familiar with metal smelting of the type performed by blacksmiths at that time. Here, I believe, he is describing a supernatural experience using concepts that he can relate to, and that his audience of the day would understand. By the way, I am not suggesting in any way that we should try to imagine what he saw and then rewrite scripture with a more technological understanding. However, we do need to realise that language has limitations. If one of us saw that vision now, we might describe it in terms of a UFO or something out of *Star Wars*.

There is an amazing section of verses (15–25) where Ezekiel describes the movement of supernatural beings and talks about wheels within wheels. Even using the language of today's advanced technology, I think we would struggle to give an adequate words-only description. Verse 18 says, 'And their rims were tall and awesome, and the rims of all four were full of eyes all around.'

In Ezekiel's time the only artificial light came from candles, torches, fires and the like. If these awesome wheel rims were surrounded by amazing bursts of light, how would Ezekiel have described them? Would he have thought of candles (which had been invented a few hundred years previously – I checked!) or would he have used the closest word he had available to what he experienced? He may have decided to use 'eyes' as being the nearest thing to describe what he saw.

A few years ago, I was chatting to an Indonesian mission worker. She had come across many Western Christians who were unhappy that God is sometimes referred to as 'Allah' in a Christian context, not just in English but in other languages. As a native English speaker, I don't refer to God as Allah in prayer or conversation (just in case you were wondering). However, I would quite happily sing a worship song in a different language that referred to God this way. Hausa, for example. My friend was quite nonplussed and said, 'What is it with these Westerners? Why are they so offended by it?' She genuinely did not get it. So I gave her this explanation.

A basic principle of difference between languages is that word-for-word equivalents are unreliable. For example, as a student I spent three months in Bulgaria. This beautiful country is the home of yoghurt. (I can't stand yoghurt. I tried to eat some to get used to it, but it just made me gag and still does.) Yoghurt is so prevalent in Bulgaria that they just call it 'milk' (*mleko*). So how do they differentiate between milk and yoghurt? Milk is *pryasno mleko* (fresh milk) and yoghurt is *kiselo mleko* (sour milk). Easy once you know, and it makes sense. They also don't have one word for cheese. There is *kashkaval*, which is hard cheese like cheddar, or *sirene*, which is like feta cheese. All cheeses are one or the other.

In Indonesian there is one single common word for God, which is used in Islam and Christianity. (I don't know if traditional religions use this word as well. They may well do.) This common word is *Ala* and you wouldn't think of using anything else. Why do we native English speakers feel awkward using it?

In the Mamprusi area of northern Ghana, where I used to work, there were Christians, Muslims and animists. All believed in God in different ways and in normal conversation would refer to Him as *NaaWuni*. *Naa* is the word for 'chief' and *Wuni* is the word for 'idol'. So 'chief idol', then. You might not like that translation but that was the word people used. And that was the word we would also use.

Anyway, back to my Indonesian friend. I explained that, in Britain at least, the word God is generally used for more than one religion, but the word Allah is a vocabulary item in English that means 'the God of the Muslims'. Hence, we would not usually use it in English in Britain in a Christian context. This went some way to putting her mind at rest.

In Malaysia a few years ago, this issue was turned on its head when some Muslims complained about Christians using the word Allah to refer to God, almost as if they were trying to copyright the word for Islam. This caused a problem for Malaysian Christians, because for hundreds of years the Malay Bible had used Allah to refer to God without a problem. The problem has now been resolved. (See resources section for more information about this.)

We might need to consider where the words for God in some European languages come from. We may find that we are happy to use words that were once assigned to pagan deities. Spanish, Italian and French, for example, use *Dios*, *Dio* or *Dieu* and sometimes the Latin *Deus*. It doesn't take much reverse engineering to see that those words derive from Zeus, the head of the Greek pantheon.

Very few of us read the Bible in its original languages. Most of us are privileged to have access to scripture in the same language that we use to talk to our loved ones and express our deepest thoughts and feelings. If we speak one of the world's major languages, we might even have a choice of versions. Some versions use high, lofty and classical language. Others can be very down to earth and informal. Some follow the word order of the original texts exactly while others try to capture the meaning of what is said. You will probably have a favourite version and that version will be different from someone else's.

Whatever version you read, something will always be lost in translation. Here are a few examples. (I'm sure you can think of many more.)

I love puns and plays on words and the Hebrew Bible is chock full of them. Sometimes, the prophets' word choices and poetry are integral to the effectiveness of these word plays. When we read the English version we have to have footnotes that explain them to us, which is a bit like a comedian having to explain why a joke is funny, i.e. the joke is no longer funny. This type of word play is lost in every language apart from the original Hebrew.

When the Israelites were supernaturally fed in the wilderness, they called the food 'manna'. Every English translation uses the word 'manna'. If you look at the footnotes they will almost always say that manna means 'what is it?', as this supernatural food was something new to the Israelites and they had no word for it. I do wonder why it has not been translated as 'thingamabob', but it has been translated as 'manna' for hundreds of years and no one is going to change that tradition.

Different languages have different levels of richness in their style and vocabulary that can be drawn on when making a translation.

If you speak more than one language, you will be aware of the limitations of each language and can switch from one to another to express something better (or if whoever you're talking to doesn't speak that language, you'll wish you could). If you're monolingual you may still have a few phrases from another language that just work better. Schadenfreude is a much more succinct way of saying 'taking pleasure in someone else's misfortune', and you might like to use it even if you don't speak German. Imagine being able to have a variety of options for phrases.

Language is very powerful and has been responsible for disagreements, church splits, and even major schisms in church history. It is easy to assume that because someone is using a different form of words, they mean something different. I have had some hilarious arguments with my wife when we were going at each other 'hammer and tongs' (whatever that means), and then we'd take a step back, think about what we were arguing about and realise that we were actually in one hundred per cent agreement but we had used different words to express what we were saying. I have a hunch that we are not the only ones this happens to.

## Questions for discussion

1. What languages do you know? Are there any words from other languages that you use?
2. Do you have a favourite translation? Could you benefit from reading more than one version of the Bible?

## Hints for leaders

Here are some non-English words and phrases familiar to many English speakers: Je ne sais quoi, the status quo, bon voyage, bon appetit, carte blanche, c'est la vie, faux pas. These are actually from French and Latin and are often used when we don't have a handy equivalent English phrase.

The notes for leaders section has a list of different Bible versions and how they differ in what can be gained from them.

# Becoming a better listener

Learning to be a better listener doesn't come naturally to most people, and certainly not to me. A standard comment from me would be to interrupt someone with, 'Let me tell you all about the listening course I've been on.' (I get looks from 'er across the room!) Sometimes I think I am listening but then I realise that all I'm doing is waiting for a pause so I can express my opinion.

So how can we become better listeners? There are plenty of guides available and I don't want to duplicate their good advice.

I would like to suggest that we cannot listen well unless we understand the person well. Often we will not be able to understand someone unless we know the meaning behind the words they are using. To take an extreme example, if someone is speaking to us in French and we don't speak French, then our understanding is very low. However, in this case it is obvious we have a problem and we need to get an interpreter. It is less obvious when we are both speaking the same language but using words in a different way. Incidentally, this is why we have to be careful on social media, as we are typing words without intonation. Even intonation can throw us. My wife has a rising tone to her 'yes', which I know in my head does not carry any additional emotional information. However, in my gut it still sounds like she is saying, 'Yes, of course I have. Stop nagging me, you stupid idiot.' She also uses 'you know' as a speech lubricant. Again, although I know this, my gut reaction is to hear, 'I don't know, otherwise you wouldn't have to tell me!'

We need to make sure we have truly understood what is being communicated to us before we respond or act on it. This can be quite difficult because sometimes asking for clarification can be perceived as a bit passive aggressive.

The sort of register we use in the way we speak can vary depending on our preference. Do we interpret all our experiences spiritually or do we prefer to express things in more emotional or psychological terms? It may well depend on how our minds work. I know myself that I have a lot of thoughts, and I need to be more discerning to know if they come from God or from my own overactive mind. Are negative thoughts always direct temptations from the evil one or just a natural result of my own emotional state? What I believe about this will influence how I communicate it.

Are we arguing about theology when we are simply using words differently? Perhaps we should take a leaf from the book of James:

My dear brothers and sisters, take note of this: everyone should be quick to listen, slow to speak and slow to become angry, 20 because human anger does not produce the righteousness that God desires. 21 Therefore, get rid of all moral filth and the evil that is so prevalent and humbly accept the word planted in you, which can save you.

22 Do not merely listen to the word, and so deceive yourselves. Do what it says. 23 Anyone who listens to the word but does not do what it says is like someone who looks at his face in a mirror 24 and, after looking at himself, goes away and immediately forgets what he looks like. 25 But whoever looks intently into the perfect law that gives freedom, and continues in it – not forgetting what they have heard, but doing it – they will be blessed in what they do.

26 Those who consider themselves religious and yet do not keep a tight rein on their tongues deceive themselves, and their religion is worthless. 27 Religion that God our Father accepts as pure and faultless is this: to look after orphans and widows in their distress and to keep oneself from being polluted by the world.

(James 1:19–27, *NIV*)

We are asked to be quick to listen. This is not at all easy. James goes on in chapter three to talk about the dangers of the tongue and says this:

> With the tongue we praise our Lord and Father, and with it we curse human beings, who have been made in God's likeness. 10 Out of the same mouth come praise and cursing. My brothers and sisters, this should not be. 11 Can both fresh water and salt water flow from the same spring? 12 My brothers and sisters, can a fig-tree bear olives, or a grapevine bear figs? Neither can a salt spring produce fresh water.

(James 3:9–12, *NIV*)

## Questions for discussion

1. What sort of questions could you ask if you would like to hear more about something without seeming aggressive?
2. Do you need to train yourself more in this area?

## Hints for leaders

If no one can think of any questions, supply some of these for comment:

- Is this similar to …? (Then talk about a similar experience that you have had or know about.)
- Could you expand a bit for my sake? I'm not sure I fully understood you.
- Could you give me some other examples of this sort of thing?

# Learning not to judge, but how?

A few years ago we adopted a Rottweiler from the local dog rescue centre (we had just trained a hearing puppy for two years and it was time to return him to Hearing Dogs for the next stage of training). I must admit we were initially prejudiced against Rottweilers, but our daughter thought it was a good idea (she had already left home at this stage, so it wasn't that she was nagging us to get one for her). So we got the dog and for ten days we wondered what on earth we had let ourselves in for. But soon our dog realised that at last she had a home and she could relax rather than go round headbutting everybody – for the first ten days or so we all had cuts on our cheekbones from where she had bashed us with her very heavy head.

I started to take her for walks round the village and often felt like I was acting out the parable of the Good Samaritan. People would cross over to the other side of the road, and I was once harangued for leaving a 'dangerous dog' outside the chemist. It didn't help that I have very short hair, my resting face is not very smiley, and I tend to walk around in a sweatshirt and trainers. I do an academic sort of job, but I don't look like an academic.

So what was going on? A lot of people (not everyone) were seeing my dog and very quickly jumping to a conclusion based on their assumptions and fears. Popular media and films have portrayed Rottweilers as dangerous and violent dogs. I think newspapers in the 1980s referred to them as 'demon dogs' and the media continues to run news stories about how they kill children. This sits deeply in the British national psyche. So, even though people saw, what was actually, a friendly dog with a friendly person this powerful narrative seemed to override the reality. Our dog, Lady, was very well trained and good-natured. She would whine pitifully when left alone for more than an hour or two and was often complimented by professional dog handlers when seen out and about. She would shake paws with new people and allow them to pet her once introduced.

You might still feel nervous around certain breeds of dog and that is OK. What I would like to reflect on is how previous learned behaviour, unconscious or not, can affect how we judge people or a situation. Jesus in Matthew 7 says the following:

Do not judge, or you too will be judged. 2 For in the same way you judge others, you will be judged, and with the measure you use, it will be measured to you.

3 Why do you look at the speck of sawdust in your brother's eye and pay no attention to the plank in your own eye? 4 How can you say to your brother, 'Let me take the speck out of your eye,' when all the time there is a plank in your own eye? 5 You hypocrite, first take the plank out of your own eye, and then you will see clearly to remove the speck from your brother's eye.

(Matthew 7:1–5, *NIV*)

This seems like an impossible standard. I cannot live up to this, and neither can any of us. Jesus gives us something to aim for, knowing that we will not achieve it. However, I don't think that means we shouldn't even try. 'Wounds from a sincere friend are better than many kisses from an enemy,' says Proverbs (27:6, *NLT*). To get to the point where we are sincere friends with someone takes time, experiencing things together, and reaching a place where we trust one another and can share such things as secrets, hopes and fears. I know there are very few people in my life with whom I can have this level of friendship. I also know that if someone like that wanted to correct me in some way, they would be able to do it with the best of intentions.

That is 'removing the speck of dust' in a figurative sense. Now if I had an actual speck of dust in my eye, I would be happy for someone to say, 'I see you have a speck of dust in your eye. Would you like me to get it out for you?' If I trusted that person I would be fine for them to do it. But that is purely for medical reasons. What Jesus is talking about here, is for us to make some kind of moral or spiritual correction.

I venture to suggest that very few of us could honestly say that we have dealt with all of our issues. We are all hypocrites if we make any attempt to judge others before we have reached a point where they can trust us fully.

## Questions for discussion

1. How well do you need to know someone before you can correct them?
2. Can you help without judging? What would that look like? What would have to happen first?
3. What assumptions and learned behaviours lead you to judge certain categories of people?

## Hints for leaders

Q1. Clarify that this is moral or spiritual correction. If your employee had not followed procedure of course you would correct them. Q2. I would suggest that as a bare minimum someone should have had some experience in their own life dealing with the particular issue they wish to help with. Even this may not be sufficient. The way an individual has dealt with whatever issue they are facing may be different to the way another should do so.

Those who wish to help someone else in this way could ask themselves the following questions: does that person trust me? Do they know me? Have I experienced life with them? If they cannot answer yes to these questions, I'm not sure it would be a good idea to get involved. I would suggest this is a dilemma to take away and ponder over.

# Practical lessons from Romans 14

It might be useful to get some guidance by having a closer look at one passage of scripture. Let's unpack Romans 14 in more detail. I'm going to suggest you read the whole chapter in any version you like. I have used the *NIV*. This is not my favourite translation, but it is more literal. Typically, Paul includes his teachings on how to live towards the end of his letters, preceded by stuff about how amazing God is (sorry, I mean his theological reflections). In this chapter the questions for discussion are within the text rather than at the end.

> Accept the one whose faith is weak, without
> quarrelling over disputable matters.

How often do you like to correct someone whose 'faith is weak'. What does that mean anyway? Not knowledgeable? Still following too many Jewish laws? Still unable to trust God fully with their life?

> 2 One person's faith allows them to eat anything, but
> another, whose faith is weak, eats only vegetables.

This is from an era where the whole vegan debate was a non-issue. So rather than try and argue whether vegans are more righteous than meat eaters, let's move on.

> 3 The one who eats everything must not treat with
> contempt the one who does not, and the one who
> does not eat everything must not judge the one who
> does, for God has accepted them.

Does that need any further explanation?

> 4 Who are you to judge someone else's servant? To
> their own master, servants stand or fall. And they will
> stand, for the Lord is able to make them stand.

A verse written in an age when almost everyone was either a master or servant, and it would have been understood much better in the time – but surely we can grasp the principle of not judging.

> 5 One person considers one day more sacred than
> another; another considers every day alike. Each of
> them should be fully convinced in their own mind.

I have seen Christians verbally rip each other apart over this and condemn Christian sportspeople for playing on Sundays.

6 Whoever regards one day as special does so to the Lord. Whoever eats meat does so to the Lord, for they give thanks to God; and whoever abstains does so to the Lord and gives thanks to God. 7 For none of us lives for ourselves alone, and none of us dies for ourselves alone. 8 If we live, we live for the Lord; and if we die, we die for the Lord. So, whether we live or die, we belong to the Lord. 9 For this very reason, Christ died and returned to life so that he might be the Lord of both the dead and the living.

10 You, then, why do you judge your brother or sister? Or why do you treat them with contempt? For we will all stand before God's judgment seat. 11 It is written:

"'As surely as I live,' says the Lord,

"every knee will bow before me;

every tongue will acknowledge God.'"

12 So then, each of us will give an account of ourselves to God.

Have you lived up to your own standards? If we are honest, most of us can't even do that.

13 Therefore let us stop passing judgement on one another. Instead, make up your mind not to put any stumbling block or obstacle in the way of a brother or sister. 14 I am convinced, being fully persuaded in the Lord Jesus, that nothing is unclean in itself. But if anyone regards something as unclean, then for that person it is unclean. 15 If your brother or sister is distressed because of what you eat, you are no longer acting in love. Do not by your eating destroy someone for whom Christ died. 16 Therefore do not let what you know is good be spoken of as evil. 17 For the kingdom of God is not a matter of eating and drinking, but of righteousness, peace and joy in the Holy Spirit, 18 because anyone who serves Christ in this way is pleasing to God and receives human approval.

19 Let us therefore make every effort to do what leads to peace and to mutual edification.

Verses 13 to 19 seem to be well fitted for the society we now live in. I often see Christians bemoaning the 'state of the world', but often the solutions that are offered look like 'turning back the clock'. If we could go back to the past we would see that Christians then were just as imperfect as they are now, but in different ways. There are stories of Victorian mill owners who would build a chapel for their workers and expect them to go there on their only day off. And thought they were being right-eous doing so. Meanwhile children were working in their factories at the risk of their lives.

> 20 Do not destroy the work of God for the sake of food. All food is clean, but it is wrong for a person to eat anything that causes someone else to stumble. 21 It is better not to eat meat or drink wine or to do anything else that will cause your brother or sister to fall.

> 22 So whatever you believe about these things keep between yourself and God.

I guess this is why I have not talked too much about actual theological and practical differences in perspective.

> Blessed is the one who does not condemn himself by what he approves. 23 But whoever has doubts is condemned if they eat, because their eating is not from faith; and everything that does not come from faith is sin.

Elsewhere in his writings, Paul refers to believers as 'ministers of reconciliation' ('All this is from God, who through Christ reconciled us to himself and gave us the *ministry of reconciliation.*' 2 Corinthians 5:18, *ESV*, italics mine). It's almost as if here in Romans he gives us a road map of how to actually do that.

## Hints for leaders

Although the questions for discussion are in the body of the chapter, I would suggest reading through the whole chapter and then going back to the questions, as this will help to put things in context.

# Notes for leaders

## Purpose of the book

When you are reading out what people's reactions might be to the statement 'we are all heretics', it might help to have some Post-it notes ready. Distribute a couple of these to each person and ask them to write one word describing their emotions. This will help you to gauge how the group is going to engage with the content. If there are quite a few negative feelings you will know to proceed gently, but if there is a lot of excitement you can press on enthusiastically. You can also use mentimeter.com to make a word cloud if everyone prefers to use their phones.

## Your struggles are different from other people's

You may get some very general, bland or closed answers to the discussion questions. Be affirmative about all the answers you get. Ask people to be more specific and take time for people to come up with answers. As more people respond, others will be reminded of what happened to them. For example, a participant in one of my groups told us that it was love that brought people to faith. We then explored different ways in which love was earthed out (i.e. in which theoretical love was expressed in practice). You can expect to spend a good thirty minutes on this discussion.

## Chart your belief: how our perspectives vary

This chapter is probably the one most likely to generate heat rather than light. If you think your group might go off on tangents it might work to look at it later after other chapters.

## The Bible is one book for all people in all ages

This chapter is quite likely to have some ideas that people might not have thought about much. We are creatures of time and space, and yet God is eternal. For people who don't like a lot of reading, there is plenty of useful Bible background material at www.bibleproject.com.

## Are you monocultural or intercultural and why does it matter?

To follow the band, look up #resonancebanduk, and to follow my own music just search for 'worshiper tom'.

## The limitations of language

If people use a more literal version of the Bible suggest they try to read something more freely translated or vice versa. If they are used to a more focused version (e.g. *The Passion Translation* or Catholic Bible) get them to read something more general. Here is a selection of English Bibles from the myriad versions available, ranging from literal to more freely translated: *King James Version, English Standard Version (ESV), New International Version (NIV), Contemporary English Version, New Living Translation (NLT), The Living Translation, The Message, The Street Bible.* If you use a more literal version then you know that you are following the original languages more closely, but you may have to work harder to understand the meaning. If you use a more freely translated version, the meaning is more likely to be clear, but sometimes the translators have had to come to a decision about what something means. You may not always agree with that decision.

## Becoming a better listener

Time for personal confession: I know that I am a terrible listener. I have been actively working on improving it. I know how important it is to unity and harmony hence its inclusion as a theme.

## Learning not to judge, but how?

The answer to question one should be 'all of them'. This is a lead-in to question two.

Here are some suggested responses for question two: be a safe place where people can come for advice and help. Can you keep confidences? Can you offer advice without judging behaviour? (This is not easy!) Be like Alice Cooper's parents. During his crazy rock years in the 70s, they did not judge his behaviour and were always there for him. Alice is still a little bit crazy but is a believer. Read his autobiography *Golf Monster* for more. If you haven't heard of him, look him up or find someone else who is an unlikely believer as an example.

Suggested responses for question three: people can be divided into categories based on everything from race, nationality, class and caste to highbrow/lowbrow, dress or tastes in music. It might be safer to get people to make their own notes and then share if they are willing. If people feel there is a particular group they are judging or making general assumptions about, it might be powerful to write the name of this group on a piece of paper and then destroy it.

## Practical lessons from Romans 14

It is possible that people might go off on their hobby horses about particular issues, although I would hope if they have made it to the end of the book this would be less likely.

You might like to celebrate getting to the end of the book. What does that look like in your context?

You might like to reflect on the whole journey. You could ask questions like, 'What one thing can I take away from this experience?' or 'Is there anything I might do differently?' You may of course find that's too many questions.

# Resources for further Bible and related research

Here are some links and books mentioned in the previous chapters.

### Chart your belief: how our perspectives vary

Read the book *Sacred Pathways* by Gary Thomas for more about the nine different types of spirituality.

### Are you monocultural or intercultural and why does it matter?

For the article on Roman hairstyles, see: https://en.wikipedia.org/wiki/Roman_hairstyles

### The limitations of language

For more information about Malaysian Christians and their use of 'Allah', see:

https://www.christianitytoday.com/news/2021/march/malaysia-allah-christians-muslims-catholic-paper-high-court.html

## Becoming a better listener

Here is one suggested guide to listening skills:
https://www.lifechange.foundation/saynow/listening-skills

Tom Schwarz is a language and culture expert who spent nine years in Ghana. A brain stem stroke in 2020 has not slowed him down much. He plays keyboards, bass and guitar in a global worship band. He lives in Oxfordshire in a four-generation household with his chickens, dog and cat, all of whom are ginger.

To catch up with him on social media, search 'worshiper tom.' For the global worship band search #resonancebanduk